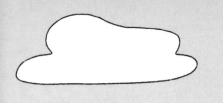

Did You Know God Created You?

By Kimberly Christensen

Illustrated By Olivia Weaver

WestBow Press books may be ordered through booksellers or by contacting:

WestBow Press
A Division of Thomas Nelson & Zondervan
1663 Liberty Drive
Bloomington, IN 47403
www.westbowpress.com
1 (866) 928-1240

Interior Image Credit: Olivia Weaver

ISBN: 978-1-9736-8245-5 (sc)
ISBN: 978-1-9736-8246-2 (e)

Library of Congress Control Number: 2019920757

Print information available on the last page.

WestBow Press rev. date: 2/26/2020

WESTBOW
PRESS®
A DIVISION OF THOMAS NELSON
& ZONDERVAN

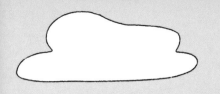

Why Is It Important For You To Read
This Book To A Child TODAY?

The earlier a child is rooted in the Authoritative Truth of God's Word about who He is, who they are, and His Wonderful plan for them, the sooner they can enjoy the Abundant Life of confidence, joy, love, hope, peace and purpose found Only In Him!

Initially providing young children with the Truth of God as Almighty Creator and Our Loving Heavenly Father establishes their foundational sense of His immense Love, Security, Value and Acceptance enabling early development of Biblically-sound minds and hearts eager to Love Him, prepared to Trust His Promises and Obey His Commands – beginning with the greatest one of all! Dispositions of Love for God and others, Thanksgiving, Joy, Praise and Prayer poise children to seek His Presence by Following His Perfect Wisdom, Will and Ways! This book is the first in the "Follow Me" series, designed to help you cultivate good ground in the little ones you love to grow in the knowledge and understanding of our Great God and Savior leading them into a life full of Confidence as His Child, Compassion for Others, and Commitment to His Will, Glorifying His Holy Name and Ready for His Return through a personal relationship with Jesus Christ.

In a world TODAY that is quickly falling further and further away from the Authoritative Truth of God's Word, this book encourages early development and demonstration of firm Christian Faith and values. Fun-loving "Sammy," named after the Bible's Samuel, and his faithful sister "Sunny," named to remind Christians to shine bright as the Lights we are called to be, teach children What it means, How it looks and Why it matters to truly be a Christian, one who Follows the example of Jesus Christ. The "Follow Me" Poem, Prayer, Pledge and Application Question engage children to begin Truly Living with Him TODAY!

With A Thankful Heart To

Our Gracious Heavenly Father
For Loving me, Saving me, and Always Protecting me

★

My parents, John and Alexis Hughes,
whose unconditional and overwhelming love
prepared me to easily receive the Love of our Heavenly Father

★

Sandy Johnson for showing me the face of a Servant's Heart

★

Genine Cooper for planting the seed of my growing Faith

★

Chaplain Dale Parker, Faith Bible College, for teaching me
the foundational Truths that lead to True Worship and
how to "think rightly about God" – Tetelestai!

★

Olivia Weaver for using her God-given artistic talent to serve
Him with the vibrant illustrations in this book.

1 Thessalonians 5:1-15

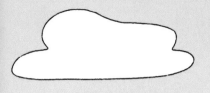

This Book Belongs To

_____

A Beloved Child of God

"My sheep hear my voice, and I know them, and they follow me. I give them eternal life, and they will never perish, and no one will snatch them out of my hand. My Father, who has given them to me, is greater than all, and no one is able to snatch them out of the Father's hand. I and the Father are one." (ESV)
John 10:27-30

For I know the plans I have for you, declares the Lord, plans for welfare and not for evil, to give you a future and a hope. (ESV)
Jeremiah 29:11

"Hi! My name is Samuel, but you can call me Sammy!"

"And I'm Sunny!"

"It's very nice to meet you!"
"Can we ask you a question?"

Did You Know
God Created You?

2

He made you
from head

to toe!

Long before
you were born,

He knew how
you would grow.

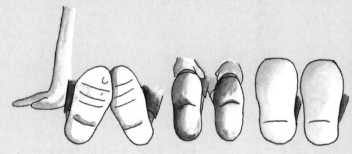

He decided
what size shoe you'd wear,

how **tall** you'd be,
and the color of your hair ….

and your eyes,
and your
skin tone too.

He chose
your nose, your ears, your mouth
and even your belly button – it's true!

You are **His**
Special Design,
One of a kind,
Created from Love by the Divine!

And what about the things you cannot see .....
like how you think or how you feel,

what's on your mind, or in your heart?

Well, that's not a tricky part

Because **God** made you inside too!

He made you to be kind, confident and strong, and He wants you to make friends and get along.

He wants you to be
patient and to be nice,

to be thoughtful,
helpful and polite.

He wants you to do what's good
and to do what's right,

to say your prayers

in the morning …. and at night.

He wants you to be respectful and thankful, to say please and thank you.

But, most of all, we have one very important thing to do…..

Love
Him
with all our heart,

and all the other people He created too! 14

They are not the same
as you.
There are many differences
to view,

but **God** created them too!

He Loves them,

He Loves me,

and **He**
Loves you!

Look all around you. It's easy to see

Just how different **God** made us to be.

But, that's ok!

No matter what anyone may say,

He wanted it exactly that way!

We are ALL **His** valuable treasures!

He Loves us
Beyond ALL measures!

We are ALL very important
to Him!

We are ALL **His** beloved
children!

He Loves us ALL the same!

He knows each and every
one of us by name!

Now that you know **God** created you,

and **He** Loves You, and Me, and Others too,

and you know what **He** wants you to do .....

Can you think of a way TODAY to begin?
What can you do
to be kind and nice and make a friend?

We only have to remember one thing.

We may
look
different,

but we are ALL
the same!

So every
single morning,  we must simply Pray

"Thank you God for creating
me and giving me this day.
Thank you for your Love and for
your Protection from up above.
TODAY, I look forward
to what I must do –
make a new friend for me and for You!
In Jesus' name I Pray. Amen."

The End ......

Is just a
New Beginning!

"Follow Me" Poem

Follow me and you will see
The way that life is meant to be
We'll learn to smile and enjoy the day
Even when things aren't going our way
We'll look at the side that's joyful and bright
And we will always shine a light
By doing what God says is good and right
And saying our prayers both morning and night.

1 Thessalonians 5:16-18
Rejoice always, pray without
ceasing, give thanks in all
circumstances; for this is the will
of God in Christ Jesus for you. (ESV)

John 14:6
Jesus answered, "I am the
way and the truth and the life.
No one comes to the Father
except through me." (ESV)

John 10:10
"The thief comes only to steal and kill
and destroy. I came that they may have
life and have it abundantly. (ESV)"

Titus 2:14 * Matthew 5:14

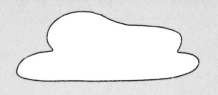

"Follow Me" Pledge

I know my Heavenly Father God loves me
And His Son Jesus Christ does too
You died on the cross to give me
The chance to live forever with you
Your Holy Spirit will guide me
And teach me all that is right and true
He will help me become who you created me to be
By helping me start anew!
I love you God with all my heart, and mind
and soul, and might, and I long to see your face too
So I will live each day
as you say
And promise to grow, trust, believe, and choose
to always only Follow you.

John 8:12
Again, Jesus spoke to them, saying,
"I am the light of the world.
Whoever follows me will not walk in darkness,
but will have the light of life." (ESV)

2 Corinthians 5:17
Therefore, if anyone is in Christ,
he is a new creation.
The old has passed away;
behold, the new has come. (ESV)

Psalm 118:24
This is the day that the Lord has made,
let us rejoice and be glad in it. (ESV)

1 Peter 2:24 * 1 Corinthians 6:19-20 * 1 John 2:6, 4:9 * John 16:13

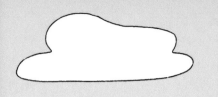

An Invitation For "Big Kids" To Redeem The Time With more Scripture verses and Hymns/ Songs that inspired this book:

Genesis 1:1,26-28; 2:7

Mark 12:30-31; 8:31-38; 4:1-20

1 Samuel 16:7

1 Corinthians 13:1-13

Romans 5:8; 8:28-29; 10:1-13; 11:36; 12:1-2

Proverbs 3:1-18; 14:12; 9:10

Ephesians 2:8-10; 4:29-32; 6:10-18

2 Corinthians 5:1-21; 6:2

Psalm 1, 19, 23, 28:7, 139:13-16

Revelation 4:8-11

Micah 6:8

Hebrews 11:1-7; 4:12

Acts 17:24-25

Matthew 5:1-16; 6:5-34; 7:1-29

Colossians 1:9-23; 3:1-16

Titus 2:11-14

Luke 9:23-27; 18:9-30; 23:26-56

Philippians 2:1-16; 4:4-9

James 1:1-27

2 Timothy 2:1-26; 3:1-17

John 3:16-17; 8:1-36; 14:15; 15:4-27

Galatians 2:20; 5:22-23

Jeremiah 4:4; 17:5-12

2 Peter 3:9

"I Have Decided To Follow Jesus"

"O Holy Night"

"Hallelujah, King of kings and Lord of lords"

"I'll Live For Jesus"

"How Great Thou Art"

"Joy To The World"

Author's Note

Thank you for taking the time to read this book to the child/children in your life! I am passionate about sharing this message of God's Truth with as many children as possible, as early as possible, and consider any opportunity to read, speak or participate in a special event a wonderful privilege. Let's protect and prepare the hearts and minds of our little ones today and help them live abundant lives full of confidence as His children, compassion for others, and commitment to His perfect will!

I look forward to hearing from you soon,

Kimberly Christensen
kimberlychristensenbooks@yahoo.com

Proverbs 22:6
Train up a child in the way he should go; even
when he is old he will not depart from it. (ESV)

Romans 10:17

Printed in the United States
By Bookmasters